*"Ruth exposes her own, often p_
Coop and offers you the reader practical tips on how to cope
with the transitional period all parents go through when their
children leave home."*

**Brandon Bays - Internationally Best-selling Author of The
Journey, The Journey for Kids and Freedom Is**

*"This book gives an invaluable insight into all that can happen when our
children 'fly the coop' written from the heart, from first hand
experience, from the pain, the reality and the truth from what was, to
what is, to what can be!*

*We are taken gently and with exquisite compassion thru' the steps of
transition and given practical suggestions and examples to guide us and
bring us the freedom to revel in who we are! now! at this moment in our
lives!*

*We can truly acknowledge and ultimately celebrate ourselves – with all
the discovered aspects of what new directions we might take, what we
can achieve, what we can change and how we can bring about those
changes – we are shown the glorious possibilities of choice!"*

Tricia Hudson - Holistic Therapy Practitioner

*"Very authentically and movingly written. Words full of WISDOM and a
worthy companion for all parents whose children have also just left
home."*

Romana Cetin

Flown the Coop

A Guide to dealing with Transition when the Kids leave Home

Ruth Bleakley-Thiessen

Also by Ruth Bleakley-Thiessen: *"Woman Rise and Shine"*

All books can be found at www.ruth-bleakley-thiessen.com/books/

ISBN-13: 978-1542529631
ISBN-10: 1542529638

For the wonderful souls who chose me as their mother

CONTENTS

Introduction   i

1 Having Kids   3

2 Being a Parent   9

3 Stepping into Change   19

4 Crisis and Transition   29

5 Transition for the Kids   53

6 Learning from others   59

7 What comes now?   75

Epilogue   87

About the Author   89

More Books by the Author   90

INTRODUCTION

A whirlwind hit my life three years ago.

At least it felt like it. My three kids all left home, flew the coop, and left behind an empty nest.

I guess either the same has happened to you or it is about to happen in the near future. So you're also being reorganized, rewoven, repatterned, just like I was.

Some events in life change us, even when we don't want the change. Circumstances change individuals, yet we are often so caught up in the event that we aren't able to respect how it happens and what it does to us. In our response to what life offers us we can become overwhelmed.

Some things deserve more time and space in our collective conversations. One of them is what happens when the kids are gone, and the way life changes us. This is a time when there is a lot to grieve and a lot to celebrate. This is a time when we consider how we are going to reshape our lives and our futures. It's a time when we bring more attention to our thoughts on what we want to change, and how we can go about the change we would like to bring about. It is important that we give ourselves the space needed to go through this extremely important phase in our life.

It can be a time without clarity. It certainly was a time of reorganization for me. A transition period. It wasn't a swift, active movement from A to B, it was a sort of a mixture, when transition took place in the midst of messiness, mushiness and confusion. When the kids leave home, your life gets rewritten. It is a huge adjustment.

In my experience I felt like I was being washed over by the waves, like I had entirely given up my control to the sweeping tide. In surrendering to the process I let go of my old self and allowed myself to write the next chapter in my life. For some of us, this same transition happens with gentle tears, or a few sobs, or a wink goodbye and an open hand, allowing the children to slip away. For others it's not just so easy. I have illustrated many examples in this book, which I hope will help you in your own personal transition.

After all, it's meeting yourself again, most likely your partner too, after a lot of years of parenting have flown by. Change often happens in the moment you'd least expect it to. My invitation is that you surrender to it and allow it to happen whilst reading on. I fully respect and acknowledge what you are going through and would love for you to have self-compassion and self-love for this important phase in your life.

Having Kids

Giving birth is hands-down the most intense and moving thing I have ever and most likely will ever experience. Intense is the best word I can think of to describe it, because it balances precariously on that rickety fence between out-of-this-world-sweet-crazy pleasure and all-consuming pain.

I've had three babies. They were all born naturally, or by spontaneous vaginal delivery (SVD), as the medical world puts it so poetically. And still, each birth was completely different.

I'll try to explain, all being from a woman's side of things. Naturally men experience the birth of their children as a moving experience too, albeit from a different perspective.

First, let me qualify the pain part. Because this is the thing most of us have been led to associate with giving birth to babies. And fear of pain is what most of us have. We don't like having our bodies hurt in any way, and this is the reason why caesarean and medicalised birth statistics are as shockingly high as they are in the developed, private medical-care funded world that is.

I've done it three times. The first time I had no idea of what it would be like, apart from what I had read in books and what my midwife had explained to the prenatal class I went to. It seems that when you're pregnant, no-one wants to scare you with the fact that childbirth is so damn painful. It's not really that I was told that giving birth would be in a heartbeat, and there is no way that anyone can say in advance how a birth is going to be anyway. The moments of my children's births are still intoxicating memories for me, as they definitely are still vivid for my husband too, who was looking on from the outside, and fevering with me as only a father can for his own flesh and blood.

I mean intoxicating because I honestly felt like I had been given the strongest happy-drug in the world when I had my children. It's incredible what hormone surges can do for you. I have never felt as powerful in all my life as I did in the seconds, minutes and hours after I birthed my children. Even after hours and hours of being in labour and a sleepless night, I felt unconditional love for all of my babies after their birth. I can remember holding each of them in my arms for the very first time, overwhelmed at the sweet beings I had given birth to just a few moments earlier. I wasn't able to do anything else other than lie gazing at them, taking in the beauty and wonder of what I had been carrying in my womb for all those months.

In fact, the post-birth high lasted for almost a week every time. I felt like Superwoman. I had just birthed a baby. In those final minutes the most primal part of me took over completely. I can remember the sound of my own voice as I pushed them out in the last visceral effort, like a goddess which took root inside of me, allowing nature to take it's course. And there they were.

My body took over from my mind. I had done what generations of women before me had done and will continue to do. After their birth I tasted life in its most concentrated form. Pure, potent and simply miraculous.

I would not exchange these experiences for all the riches in the world.

If you have carried life within your body and given birth, you will have had your own innate experience. For me, the first birth started delicately, after having to lie flat on my back for four weeks with premature contractions. My first son wanted to come early but wasn't allowed to for his own good, so the doctor said. I had been put onto medication to prevent a premature birth. This was a bit of a bummer, as I wasn't the most patient of expectant mothers. So after four weeks of close communication with the child in my womb, my husband and I agreed to allow him to come any time after two weeks before the due-date arrived, which was considered a normal time to deliver.

And he wanted to come immediately after my medication was stopped. My contractions started, which were painful, more painful than pain as I knew it. My husband accompanied me to the hospital and the midwife sent me away to walk so that my cervix would dilate more. I remember sitting and moving inside the car, puffing through the contractions. Then I was allowed to relax in the bath before going into the delivery ward. I guess this was a normal birth, which took about eleven hours.

I'll never forget his most exquisitely beautiful face with long black hair surrounding his features. The midwife called him Mickey Mouse, which with his black hair, he did sort of resemble.

The second birth was completely different. I was woken up at two in the morning with contractions. It was ten days before my due-date. This child had been more active during the pregnancy, kicking a lot. We got someone in as arranged to look after our first son and we drove to the hospital. I wanted to lie in a warm bath again to allow nature to open my cervix in a relaxing manner. No way, they pushed me into the delivery room as the baby was already well under way. It went like a storm. He was there with only two pushes at five o'clock in the morning. We thought, wow, this little guy knows what he wants, and he has gone through most of his life in this manner since.

The third time I got out of bed in the morning, again also ten days before my due-date. My waters broke, wetting the insides of my legs, which made me get right back into bed. I called my husband, who was getting ready to leave the house for work. I was carried out of bed and into the ambulance on a stretcher to be taken to hospital. I wasn't sure which way round the baby was lying, so I had to be careful. My other two kids slept soundly through the whole procedure, although I'm sure it would have been exciting for them to see the ambulance. After an initial examination in the hospital I was given breakfast, so that I would have enough strength for the birth, and I was sent off to climb stairs to get things going. My contractions hadn't started yet. Eventually they did, and the procedure continued until early afternoon, when our third son arrived.

We were home with him late afternoon. It all seemed so surreal at the time. I remember that there was thick snow on the ground and we had trouble getting home. When we arrived, everyone crowded around the new member of our family and he was greeted with wonder and joy.

Upon consideration, each child moved his tiny arms and legs after birth the way I had felt him move inside of my womb. Only now, they moved outside of me, with more room at last to stretch their little limbs, test their muscles, feel touch, water, clothing and the air on their tiny little bodies. I was mesmerized and totally in love.

Having spoken about my births and the pains of it, which all went very well, birth can also be a traumatic affair for the mother and the child. A lot of complications can arise. It can become a long drawn out affair. It can be a breach birth, there can be complications with the baby or with the mother, not to mention the trauma of still birth. I have been very lucky, for which I am deeply grateful. The only thing that happened to us was that I ripped internally with each birth. I guess they needed room in their birth canal. Each time I was neatly stitched up whilst holding my child in my arms. The last time I could have done with more anaesthetic, a lot more anaesthetic. I remember each and every stitch, but I was holding my newly born son in my arms, which distracted me from what was going on in that area of my body, and it made up for it.

What I didn't see, but what my husband did, who cut the umbilical cords to our children each time, was that one of our sons had his umbilical cord around his neck and was blue in his face when he was born. The cord was quickly unravelled by the midwife and all went well. It must have been quite a shock to my husband, probably for the baby too. I, of course wasn't able to see it from my position, which was good, I felt, as I was able to stay calm.

Some mothers have no problem with their bodies after birth, and bounce straight back, even liking their body more than ever as a mother. After a pregnancy it's natural that a woman's body changes. It's a very feminine stage of breast-feeding. My body felt round, soft and squishy. As mothers, we are reminded daily of what we went through to have children. Stretch marks, cellulite and a flabby belly are the least of the worries, although this is a cause for shame for a lot of women. I know one woman who had extensive physical pain as her hips were dislocated during giving birth to her son. She needed ongoing medical care and physiotherapy for years.

One point I would like to consider here is that if a birth is difficult, even traumatic, it may unconsciously affect the relationship we have to our children. What has it done to our body? What has it done to the child? In which way has it affected us? Trauma does get stored in the body if we don't deal with it emotionally. Even though the pain of giving birth will be forgotten about very quickly, hormones take good care of that themselves, a difficult birth can cause havoc in our system. I will go into this in more detail in chapter four.

Being human, we all have insecurities; we are all scarred, imperfect and flawed in some way, physically and emotionally. Life is full, and with a child, we have the sweetest little chunk who fills our heart. Instead of being proud of the changes in our body, we often forget the big why in our considerations and judge ourselves wrongly. I've always struggled to accept my flaws, but after giving birth to my sons, those flaws seem more like beautiful marks of our journey together. I pray you see yourself through the eyes of your children, they know no judgement. They know love, and they think you are beautiful, even with all of your imperfections.

If only the rest of the world could see that way too.

Being a Parent

The day of giving birth to a fresh new being is the very beginning of a whole new way of using your senses. Listening probably takes first place.

Part of the exhaustion in the first weeks of parenthood, especially for a mother, is from learning which cry means hunger, tiredness or the need to be held. It's about coming to understand which middle-of-the-night whimperings are likely to escalate and which will settle and silence themselves. It's about getting to know the personal rhythm of the baby and its personality. A mother hears the tiniest little noise from her child and wakes up from the deepest of sleeps.

It's quite natural that babies make sounds, which only mothers can at first understand. When you listen to the sounds, they become words which at first aren't able to be articulated. The words become sentences and the sentences become stories.

Later, you can smile as you listen to nursery rhymes and little songs sung wrongly, words spoken back-to-front and the humorous things that your child says. I have these gems written down in little books. My kids love to ponder through them, it brings them back so many memories, and they laugh heartily at themselves.

As a parent, you get to know the voice of your child calling you in a crowd of children. You know just by the way they speak how they are feeling. Their childish excitement is conveyed to the people they trust the most – their parents. Parents know what their kids mean more than other people do, there is a blood connection.

As a parent you learn a very important sound – that particular hum of silence that is delicious, yet can also mean that something, somewhere is not quite right.

But it is not just listening that changes with parenthood, it is all of the senses.

A parent is the taster. I held the plastic spoon and used my bottom lip or the tip of my tongue to check for too much heat, bitterness, saltiness or spice before allowing my little ones to savour their food. I licked the very last dregs off spoons. I became accustomed to the sweet strawberry-yoghurty or pungent green spinachy kisses from my children.

My sense of smell heightened, saturating every scent with feeling. I knew the exact smell of my children, especially in the soft creases of their neck, and the soft as petal and peaches on their cheek. Their scent comes back to me today if I tune in to them.

I would draw my children close to me, daring someone to blow cigarette smoke or car fumes their way. I knew the scent of all the baby care products on their skin, and of other people's cuddles too. The pungent smell of nappies didn't matter one little bit to me. I knew at the end of the day, when I smelt the sweet smell of my children, that all was okay.

Parents see everything on their children – every new graze, bump, cut, bruise or freckle. Every expression of unease, joy, excitement and happiness too.

I used to scan the places we went to - rooms, playgrounds, roads we would cross, never stopping looking for potential dangers, and only when I was sure would I let my kids skip on. At the park, the market, the playground and at other people's houses, I knew that I must start to foster independence, so I would drop little hands. But I never, for a second, let their bobbing heads out of my sight.

The touch of a parent is more powerful than I ever could have imagined. All of a sudden I realized that my cool hand on a hot forehead could relieve a lot of suffering, just as the squeeze and a rub of a recently bruised knee or grazed elbow worked wonders. My kisses and blows on tiny wounds contained magic, and there is not much that a hug cannot soothe. My second son used to only fall asleep in my bed when he was a baby with my nose between his thumb and fingers.

As the years went by, some of these senses started to feel less necessary. A pulling away of a tiny body started when I bent over to kiss. When I reached over to brush hair out of the eyes, or brush dirt from a cheek, it wasn't welcome. The sweet baby smell is long gone, replaced by earthier, saltier smells. There were fewer calls in the middle of the night. Meals became independent experiences, where there was no need to blow soups before they were ravished. A time came when I had to ask for permission for kisses.

But as a parent, you can't turn the senses off. Once started, you always sit up straight in bed at night, thinking there could be something wrong with one of the kids at the slightest noise. This new way of listening will never end, even when the kids are older.

The seeing. The tasting. The touch. I miss it. Even when they're gone.

Now I'm speaking from the perspective of a mother, which I am. There is an ideal here which mums may consciously or unconsciously try to live up to. The pure mother, full of tender love and compassion, the Mother Mary. The perfectionist. The one who struggles with her temper at times, not wanting to lose it. The one who wants to take more time to sit down and listen to her kids, just drinking in their presence. The one who would love to have more patience. The one who really wants to let them know how much she loves them, to kiss them more and show her appreciation, yet never seems to get round to it. These are some of the struggles of a normal mother.

The ideal mother is not what I was. I had lots of joy with my kids, it felt so simple, so easy. It's natural with kids, they're easy and not so spoiled and tainted as many adults have become. I'm a person who loves being in nature and who loves natural things. I loved them and I let them free. It works. I'm not perfect. Of course I made mistakes, which I hope I will be forgiven for. But it's not that I'm not satisfied enough, and think that I could have done it all better.

I have many memories of my own mother when I was small. We would sit in front of the fire when it was cold outside, me cuddled up on her knee. My mum was beautiful to me. She was the one who looked after me and loved me a lot. I felt her closeness, her unique smell. I knew deep down that she would love me forever and beyond it. There was a connection to her that I don't believe I have ever found with any other human being. I loved her treats, going shopping with her, her own sense of fun, her singing, her own way of saying "I love you". All that I am I owe to my mother. I attribute my success in life to the moral, intellectual and physical education I received from her. And to honour my father, of course I learned a lot from him too.

Where would I be without all that love? If there is anything on this earth that is sacred, it is motherhood. No one can explain the magic that occurs when a woman knits together an unseen spirit from the Other Side with the perfection of a human body inside her womb. One woman told me that she first found out what it is to love when she had had her son.

What alchemy occurs when a mother hears her crying infant and she lets down her milk? What mystery is it that her milk changes to suit the needs of her child with every feeding?

How are we to explain that when our child is born, we can pick them out by their scent in a roomful of babies?

How are we not to be broken by the unwavering, unconditional trust of the toddler who lifts his eyes and small, trembling hand towards his mother, knowing that she will understand his tears?

What can take hold of a woman's heart more strongly than the need to protect her child from all harm? Would she not walk through fire and risk death to shield her flesh and blood from danger? Mothers think twice, once for themselves and once for their children.

Women are the human embodiment of our Mother Earth. Living and dying with every breath that their children take, mothers give their entire body over to the preservation of humankind. And yet, some women are ashamed of the role we take as caregivers to the planets greatest gift and resource... our children. It's often not respected for the work it is. Biology is the least of what makes someone a mother. No matter how a woman came about to motherhood, whether through pregnancy, adoption, fostering, or fate, they are the lifeline of everything that is. This is a reason for gratitude.

Children are the best teachers we can have by far. I cannot express that enough, and how right I have found this to be. Having children for me has been an incredible growth experience. Small children are like cosmic mirrors, constantly reflecting every emotion and thought pattern we show them. They learn from their peers by seeing and doing, by imitation. Often parents are led to reflect exactly what their own values are, and what they believe is worth teaching their children. I have been unconsciously forced to take a look at how I would like the world to be, so that my children can have a life worth living. Children bring out the best in people, bearing their souls and opening people's hearts just a little more with their innocence and boundless joy.

When you hold a little baby, you can sense and see the pureness they have, not yet formed to do something or be someone just to get a little love and appreciation from their family. Even babies have huge unique personalities already in place, which will be carved out more throughout life.

As a mother, I didn't want my children to feel left alone. I worked from home and enjoyed looking after them. And then they grew up. I used to hear other people saying that time flies by so quickly, the kids are gone before you know it. Now I hear myself saying the exact same thing.

When my first son finished school, living in Germany, he absolved his compulsory year of civilian service, as he decided he didn't want to go to the army. He then applied for a place at a university near us to study at and whilst waiting, did two separate hands-on-training at a local radio station.

To his frustration, he kept getting refusals from the university, so after a while he decided that he would have to look further afield for a university, if he was going to get anywhere.

After applying for a number of places to study, from which three acceptances came at the same time, he was forced to decide which one to accept. So he headed off for the opposite end of the country. My husband drove him with his bags and pack. The car was full, so I stayed at home. It was a huge move for my son at that time, as he really didn't want to go so far away. Needless to say, fate had other plans for him and he's now finished his studies and has moved back not quite so far away. Looking back, it really has done him good.

But he wasn't the first to go. Our second son had just finished school and was ready and willing to go out into the big wide world to see what it holds. Being a person who knows what he wants and goes for it, he applied for a gap year to do voluntary work in the social sector. He ended up in France working in a hostel for homeless men. He was extremely brave in my eyes, and it was his choice. Or if you believe in it, the universe pushed him in this direction, for whatever reason we will find out.

So a few weeks after he'd finished school, he handed us his keys to the house and left. That was a few months before his brother left.

The younger son soon realized that he wasn't keen on being the last child at home. He was missing his brothers. He had also just finished school and had plans to move to a nearby city to live with a few close friends in a shared apartment. They all planned to do the same thing. They found work in kindergartens and did a voluntary year with children.

The LAST one. My full time job as a professional mother came to an end. Between my full-time days of cooking, school things, driving them here and there, homework patrol, I was always busy with "them", with not so much time for "me". Years of stuffed passions and desires wedged into my core.

Gone.

Flown the coop.

The empty nest.

It had taken five years to have them all. Now they were gone within nine months.

It was damn quiet at home, which fell like a brick on me. I was working from home at that time, having just given up my studio due to dampness and an increasing problem of mould on the walls.

It all happened so quick, my husband and I had difficulties dealing with the suddenness of it all. I'd wander into empty rooms looking for a purpose. Searching for a new role. Everything hit a nerve. I felt a little lost. We both had our own methods of dealing with it. We got caught up in our own activities to dull the realization that the kids really were gone, two of them far away. No blame for that, I did it on my parents too. In fact, I moved out of home the same year as my grandmother passed on and my older brother got married. I had no idea of what I did to my mother, as I just didn't think about how she felt at the time. As a young person, you are pulled by where you think you should be and what you feel you have to do. You don't lose a thought about how your parents feel. At least I didn't. I know that she cried bitterly that Christmas as she was missing so many people at the same time.

Then our cat died a few months later. She had seen the boys grow up and had been a companion to all of us. She had reached the ripe old age of seventeen, which isn't bad for a cat. As you can guess, you could hear a pin drop in the house during the daytime now.

Stepping into Change

My husband was on a four day, cross-country trip with our son, the car full of pieces of furniture, utensils, books and clothes belonging to him, driving from the top of Germany to the very bottom of it to get him settled into his new life as a student. He'd never lived that far away from home. I'm so excited for him, seeing his capability, strength and determination to make something out of himself, the way he wants to do it. I feel how proud I am for him, even as I grapple with this new emptiness in my nest.

Feeling the new experience of this heartbreakingly intense mother love, the attachment and the freedom I want him to have, both at the same time, his, mine and my husband's, as two sides of one beautiful coin. My man was enjoying those precious moments of laughter, connection, boredom, and their endless supply of music as they drove down the autobahn. They were probably trying not to think about the goodbye.

Often one of the very first words parents say to their children is "No". We don't want a child to touch anything that might hurt them, so they will say "No". As kids grow into their teen-aged years, they want to spread their wings, yet the parents consider the dangers involved in activities planned before the teens do. Parents still want their children to be safe, so many times they continue to say "No". Is it any wonder that "No" gets to be a habit? What would happen if we decided to change the negative response and practise saying "Yes" instead?

"No" is a word that closes doors and may keep you from some of life's greatest opportunities. "Yes" opens doors. As you practise saying "Yes", more comes to you. People you have kept at an arm's length show up to assist you. Relationships improve. Every day opens up new possibilities. Once you throw out an area of acceptance, life itself wants to give it to you. You have opened up a space to be filled with good.

So if we say "Yes" to what our children want to do when they get older, it helps them on their way, it allows doors to be opened for them and it helps them know that they are accepted and loved.

We can't get round it anyway, nor can we stop it, so it's easier to say "Yes" to change and to what the kids want and just let them go and get on with it.

My mother was very good at this. She let me make my own experiences and learn from them. It was much better than fighting over things, even though I was up to things my brothers didn't do, and my mother never did. I respect her a lot now for

Judgement

Parents have expectations and concepts about how children

should be and what they should be doing. We want the best for them in life. Some parents have the desire that the children make up for what they weren't able to achieve within the span of their own lifetime. The offspring are expected to go for the dream job, be successful, happy, find a partner where it really works for them, attain wealth and comfort in life, travel, and all at the same time. When these concepts and expectations aren't fulfilled, judgment may arise, as can resentment.

Children also have expectations on their parents. They need to know that they are supported in the best way their parents are able to support them. For some this is the possibility of studying, for another it is emotional support.

Judgement can cause tension and separation. How often do you put judgment on yourself or on someone else? This is a trap. Just imagine what the world would be like if we stopped judging ourselves and other people.

If any of our problems or hardships take us in any way away from joy, they can bring us closer to love in the end. Joy and love come in a double pack. The letting go of concepts, expectations or of the control we believe we have over our children is a process. We tend to put a lot of pressure on ourselves in trying to control the outcome of things. And we have pressure put onto us to fulfil the expectations of others.

When I was young, I was made to go to piano lessons, although I didn't particularly want to go, and I had no particular talent at all for playing the piano. My great aunt happened to be a music teacher, and she lived not so far from us, so my brothers and I were given the chance of learning to play the piano. A wonderful chance which other children would grasp at, but I didn't want to, and I rebelled against it sooner or later. There was an unexpressed sadness, and a feeling of shame and guilt that my parents didn't let me grow up and be just as I am. I didn't want to question what they wanted me to do, as I obviously wanted to feel loved, and I was scared that they would withdraw their love if they knew how I felt about the piano lessons. This put me in the position where I felt like being in a prison, lost, put under pressure, with no energy and denying the person I really was. My parents were totally unaware of all of this.

When I processed and let go of it in a therapy session, a huge amount of softness, self-compassion and femininity came back to me.

The same thing happened to a client of mine, who, as a little girl, was forced to go to ballet classes and didn't really want to. At the time she felt imprisoned, lost and estranged. She felt no joy going to these classes but she was afraid to admit it to her parents for a long time, as she wanted to please them and was scared of their reaction if she refused to learn ballet. It was an inner conflict.

Children are well capable of listening to their inner intuition. In fact, they're usually closer to it than we think. It's important that we as parents give them permission to drop something when they aren't comfortable with it, instead of forcing things on them that we think would be good for them. Kids have to be able to say "No" just as much as adults do. Sometimes it takes a little bit of discernment on all sides. There is no blame to be had or taken anywhere, it's just a matter of being able to stand up for yourself at any age, and being allowed to do so. It strengthens the voice and the character in the end.

If you find yourself somehow judging your child, a good way to deal with it is to ask yourself the following questions:

"What invention am I using to judge my children?"

"What need for validation am I choosing to get what I want from my children?"

"What invention am I using to never accept how my children are?"

"What invention am I using to never let my children be happy just as they are?"

"What expectations am I holding that's causing a deficit to a loving relationship with my children?"

Contemplate for a while on these questions. If anything comes up for you, let it go. It's possible to drop your concepts and expectations within a split second. This exercise will do wonders for the relationship between parents and their children. After all, everyone just wants to be as they are, to be loved, respected, accepted, and to find loving support within the family. It's one of the most important things in life.

The change at midlife

Stepping into change when the children leave home usually happens around the time when you are in the middle of your life. This is also the time when your hormones change and your body starts to show signs of change. Both men and women experience either subtle or significant physical and emotional changes at midlife, it's a normal part of life. So there's a lot of change happening on several levels, which is not to be underestimated.

The physical changes can have even more significant consequences on a person's life than those that happen at puberty, but most of us are not even slightly prepared for them! You have a sense that something is changing in your body, but it's not exactly clear what is changing. At midlife, it's not just sex hormones that are changing. Your adrenal hormones, thyroid hormones, and even insulin (a hormone that regulates blood sugar) can change with significant consequences to your life.

Here are just a few of the things that can happen as a result of midlife hormone changes:

• Sleep problems

• Weight gain

• Libido changes

• Hair loss

• Greying hair

• Skin changes

• Headaches

• Irritability

• Eyesight changes

• Brain fog

• Difficulty concentrating

• Hot flashes

• Mood changes

Your body is changing, but each person is different. Just as in puberty, midlife affects each person differently. Some kids reach puberty earlier than others; at midlife some people feel the

effects sooner than others. At puberty some kids experience brand new physical and mental health problems; that's also true for people at midlife. Some kids have a tougher time at puberty than others; the same is true at midlife. You just can't predict what will happen to you, or how it will affect you. Maybe you're not sleeping as well and as much as you used to. Maybe you can't eat the same way as you used to without gaining weight. Maybe your libido is changing.

Of course women go through significant hormonal changes during midlife as they go through perimenopause and menopause. Although men think that these timely hormone changes just affect women, that is absolutely not true. Men also experience midlife hormonal changes.

At this time in your life there is transformative power in change, especially the phase when your children fly the coop. This is the time when you have more time for yourself to unlock the wisdom inside of yourself. A lot of the demands of being a parent fall away from you. The daily routine changes. There is empowerment over obligation. Just as a caterpillar dissolves to re-form as a butterfly, you shape shift during this time to transform and gain access to a mature wisdom, knowing that this will grow stronger and stronger.

Conscious change

Everything has a beginning and an ending. If we make our peace with that, it makes change much easier to accept and embrace. A strong attachment to the past can show up as an unwillingness to face the present reality. We suffer, and we make others suffer too by trying to hold onto things after their time, whether it's relationships, experiences, or just the previous moment. Accepting the true transient nature of things eases our fears, opens our hearts, and benefits ourselves and others. Non-attachment is neither indifference nor self-denial. Ironically, letting go of attachment is the secret to really enjoying life and loving others. It is freedom.

Contrary to popular belief, you CAN choose how to step into change. You can either wait for the symptoms to strike, or you can consciously enter this pivotal rite of passage with curiosity, grace, an open heart, irreverent humour and with lots of support and guidance.

When you do, you're saying no to the limiting view of change. You're choosing instead to engage with your desires, your dreams, your well-being, your wisdom and the next phase in the life of your children. It doesn't mean that your value as a parent diminishes, everyone can grow here.

This is stepping into change consciously. Let's explore this a little further.

If change means inconvenient symptoms, conscious change moves beyond managing change to discover the changes your soul wants you to make.

If stepping into change makes you afraid, consciously changing is a choice to engage in discovering what's truly possible in this part of your life.

If stepping into change makes you feel helpless and out of control, consciously stepping into change holds you accountable for your own well-being — including your commitment to harness the potency of this time of transformation.

If stepping into change when the kids leave home makes you want time to stand still, consciously stepping into change embraces The Change — you revamp beliefs, update your relationships and get into enjoying your life.

Let's meet this change with barefaced, courageous honesty and compassion and share its life-giving charm with our kids.

Crisis and Transition

One of the hardest things for most parents I have spoken to is that after years upon years of bringing up their children in the best way they thought possible, instead of feeling joy now that they have flown into the wide world, they feel sad, anxious, or even depressed, faced with a hole and unable to enjoy their new found freedom.

Going through any life transition can be difficult. It can cause stress, which can paralyze our ability to cope. It can negatively affect our well-being and our ability to function as well as we would like to.

I am being reorganized by being a mother whose children have gone their own ways. To call it a major transition is to underestimate it, dramatically. I'm being reorganized, rewoven, repatterned. There is a lot to grieve in that, and also a lot to celebrate. I would call it a crisis in the beginning. My life and my future are being reshaped.

Our culture celebrates the individual who changes his or her circumstances, but we don't respect as much how certain circumstances can change us. In part, I understand that – when we overcome and respond to what life hands us, that's where the light often comes through, where courage comes in, and where goodness can triumph. And yet, there is something that deserves more time and space in our collective conversations about this other kind of experience, about the way life changes us.

In our culture we celebrate times of clarity, but do we give enough respect for their inevitable partners – the times of being unclear? I went through one of those times when being a mother without my kids reorganized me.

I found out that transition is the way to personal development. The end is where we start from, in this case the leaving of the kids, and it's a precondition of self-renewal. In the beginning of this development, I was devastated. In fact I was quite brought down to my knees in heartache and not knowing how to deal with it. There were many restless nights of sleep, followed by groundless days of searching for an anchor to tether me from blowing away in the unknown. I cried a river of tears, at first for a fortnight. Nothing was the same. Everything seemed to have changed.

After a while I found myself letting go of my old self, able to face the next chapter. To let the children go with some gentle tears, or a few sobs, or a wink and an open hand through which they can slip away is to meet our old selves again, years later, in the moment you'd least expect to. It is to surrender to change.

My role as a mother had fallen from me, at least that is what it seemed to be like. A part of my identity was gone, leaving me floundering like a fish out of water at first.

An important aspect of being a parent in change is developing the ability to let go of things that don't serve you, so that you can make room for better things to take root in your life. Let go of the control, let go of the fear, let go of all expectations and step into a bigger sense of trust. You'll know you're on your way to letting go when you feel the flow of joy and possibility enter into your life again.

This doesn't happen all at once; it's a process. And in this process you may have things arise for you, which will require you to take a deeper look at. But most things that are worth it take time and energy. And you don't have to uncover everything at once. Healing takes place layer by layer, like peeling an onion. There can be something wonderful about it and maybe also something difficult about it.

The lotus flower symbolises rebirth, renewal and spiritual awakening. This beautiful flower which effortlessly floats on top of the water really had to work hard to blossom. These wonderful flowers actually grow out of the mud at the bottom of a river or pond and have to break through the mud and then grow up to the surface where they blossom. You too can dive into your own personal mud, so to speak, and like the lotus flower rise to the surface and blossom into a wonderful new version of your self.

In order to blossom, you have to look inward and bring your attention toward removing whatever blocks are holding you back. Maybe it's a feeling of shame, guilt, fear or loneliness.

To start breaking through your own mud, here are some of the things you can do to start.

Be aware of your feelings.

From my own experience, I know that deep grief and confusion can have something to do with events which happened further back in time. I know this from my work as a coach as well. Memories of hurt or despair are awoken in our unconsciousness, maybe the loss of a loved one or a beloved pet.

It wasn't too long into my crisis that I experienced a cascade of losses going back in time. Like a deck of cards, fanned out one after another, the end of my own school time which brought with it the loss of friends who left to continue their lives elsewhere, pets dying, grandparents passing away, my brother getting married, moving out of the country I was born in, the loss of friendships, finishing art school, running out of money, the passing of my mother, break-ups and broken hearts, ending jobs and businesses, etc.. Moment after painful moment of letting go, saying goodbye and change; this is what my journey showed me. And there was this intense grief, triggered by the fact that the kids had gone, which needed to be dealt with. In my inner landscape, I felt that the disappearance of all this in my life was like battle scars which hadn't properly healed. I had been having all these losses and had not been feeling the deep despair of it all fully.

We are born knowing how to grieve, crying naturally to release tension and purge emotions. Positive expressions of our grief can be healing, whilst suppressing it can be destructive and inhibit our ability to genuinely connect with others.

Although grief is a natural process, many of us were taught from a young age to contain our feelings and to act like we're okay, even when we're not. Emotional pain and grief can be so frightening that we try to push it away and distract ourselves to avoid truly feeling it.

Each culture has its own mourning ceremonies, traditions and behaviours to express grief. In a culture where there is an absence of real ceremony, where death is not fully integrated into life, holding back strong emotions might even be considered virtuous.

We are concerned that openly letting out our sorrow will make other people feel uncomfortable. Witnessing someone else's grief can remind us of our own past losses or ones we will face in the future. By accepting our own grief we might find it easier to have empathy for another's heartache.

People sometimes try to pull themselves prematurely out of their grief, pulling themselves together before the grieving has finished. They resist it because they think that what they're experiencing is perhaps not normal, and carry thoughts about grieving that prevent real healing from occurring.

There may be pressure from friends and family, or a self-imposed expectation to move on. An "aren't you finished grieving yet?" attitude rather than "Have you grieved enough? Have you cried enough?" How long a grieving process takes is individual, there is no time-line for it. Grief is an emotion that rises deep from the soul.

By embracing our grief we have the opportunity to not only heal our deepest wounds, but also to tap into the creative force of those once-buried emotions. From this place of openness we have the power to take control of our own healing journey and inspire the world around us to do the same.

A part of me was attached to my grief, wanting to hold on to it to prove my battle scars. That's really self-torture. It involves both the mind and the body and it can take on a life of it's own. Naturally, it needed letting go of. It's when I let go of my attachment to how I think things should be, when I give up my need to control, when I don't live a life filled with expectations, and when I step into a deeper sense of trust, that's when I know I will find true freedom. And it's in this true freedom that I'm able to find security within myself, which is really important in a crisis.

Letting go, as we all know, is easier said than done. It means that a change will evidently need to take place in your life. It's often easier to stay in the sticky mud of the present, than it is to break through it like the lotus flower and blossom. There's usually a notion we have of how we think things should be. An ending of something means a letting go of an old role, a way of being, a set of beliefs or an attitude.

The most important way to deal with this crisis is awareness.

Identify that you need to let go of the kids who have just flown the coop. You're in a state of transition. You're moving from the phase when you looked after your family to the phase of looking after yourself more. And that doesn't happen without some commotion, especially from yourself, maybe also from your partner and your children. After all, everyone is used to something different. And the willingness to let go can be hard.

I felt challenged with my feelings and what I wanted from life when my kids left home. I didn't know what I wanted to do, where I wanted to be or who I wanted to do anything with.

And we can help ourselves in several ways.

Face the sadness, pain, loss, anger, guilt, whatever is there for you. Feel all the feelings that arise when you step into letting go. The important thing is that you allow yourself to fully feel your feelings, don't hold them back.

The best way to do this is to give yourself full permission to feel what is there. I mean in the present moment. I can do this best when I take a few moments for myself, sit down in a comfy chair, close my eyes and bring all of my awareness inwards to my body. Without thinking of the past or the future, feel into your body and acknowledge whatever feelings and emotions you have right now. Don't push them away, pull a lid on top of them or occupy yourself with anything else for a while. The more we resist our feelings, the stronger they will arise. They are only a part of us and long for the opportunity to be acknowledged.

I have found that if I ignore my feelings, they either arise at an impossible time, or they take on a life of their own, often even manifesting in my body as pain and stiffness. There can be times in life when we don't even realize that we aren't feeling good, as we often take to other methods to numb ourselves, like eating, watching TV or alcohol. Often when we say we're okay, we don't really mean it.

A girlfriend of mine always had the feeling that she had to function as a mother, cleaning, cooking, always ahead with her energy. She was afraid of being incompetent and doing something incorrect. She never allowed herself to cry or be angry, she was always in control, managing everything perfectly.

She functioned for her children and kept herself fit for them. She was a very understanding, enthusiastic mum. She loved her kids to pieces, always trying to bring out the best in them.

Yet she often felt very tired, rigid in her body and under pressure. She tried to protect herself and her family against hurt, against being looked upon as being a bad mother, and even against not letting the love in that was there. It cost her a lot of closeness and vulnerability, freedom and energy in her life.

She had unconsciously been trying to live her life with a lot of rules and responsibilities where she thought that she had to stay true to them all. It had caused her to become stuck in her role. When her kids left home, a whole world broke apart for her. She had to learn to live out of freedom and love in a completely different way. She had to give herself permission to nourish herself and allow life to show itself to her in a new way. She learned to embrace the change and to be a woman who is now more relaxed.

To overcome the fear of change, it's necessary to feel the fear and move forward to give birth to the new. If you feel resistance to change, just be present with it. Grieve what's no longer going to be there. That's the only way to usher all the good in when this phase has passed.

Guilt, shame and resentfulness

Guilt and resentfulness are very common among parents just after the kids leave home. These emotions are judged by us as very negative and harmful emotions. They generate a lot of doubt about your new role as what we'll call a parent in freedom. It's important to face these issues.

Some parents think that they have either been too hard or too soft on their children in their upbringing. Some wish that they should have spent more time with them when there was the opportunity. Some are actually resentful towards their children for going and leaving them. There is a whole palette of reasons for feeling guilty or resentful. It can make the parents be very hard on themselves where it's not necessary.

Indeed, feelings of resentment can set in after the birth of a child, especially if it has been a difficult birth, which has had a changing effect on your body. The toll of carrying a child and giving birth has its effects. Women can carry resentment towards their children either because of this, or because they have been robbed of their freedom. I certainly didn't know what it was like to be a mother until I was one. It was much harder than I had imagined it to be. I don't think that anyone who hasn't been through it can imagine what the joys and the sorrows are. Now I look at my bikini figure and tell myself, well I have three children for what I see. Lots of love to them!

Just the same, children can carry deeply rooted resentment for the way their birth went. Often, it's only when we are born that we realize that we have a body, in which we can feel restricted in a limiting way. There may have been pain. It may have been that there wasn't the expected welcome. That's what it's like to be human.

Guilt happens when what we think we should do or be is in direct opposition to what we really want or are. This can happen when we feel under pressure and the pressure can come from our family, from society or from some underlying belief we hold. The feeling of guilt tells us that we made a mistake. This in turn causes shame that there has been a mistake.

You need to be gentle with yourself on guilt and shame. By acknowledging that there is a part of you that needed this experience on a higher level of consciousness, for whatever you have needed to learn from it, you will be able to rid yourself of your guilt. In other words, if you have indulged, your body was telling you that you wanted to enjoy that piece of cake or that ice cream, or that afternoon away from it all. Once you acknowledge that part of yourself, you can just be yourself.

Shame is one of the most painful and heavy emotions that we can have. There is no humour or lightness in shame, it weighs heavily on our psyche. It can be released when we first of all admit to ourselves that the shame is there, and when we have the courage to talk about whatever we feel ashamed about, and are willing to receive support.

It's important to look into the reasons behind the guilt or resentment. We all do our best at any given time within the given circumstances. If for any reason this fails, or isn't up to your standard, as we are human after all and we all make mistakes now and again, ironing it out by forgiving ourselves or whoever needs it is a wonderful way of dealing with it. The willingness to stop your thoughts around shame, guilt or resentment and to forgive is your own choice.

Be good to yourself

Self-care is not selfish at this time in your life.

You had to have courage and faith in having your children. You also have to embrace trust in the inevitable change. Get to know yourself again in a new way. When the role of being a mum or dad falls away at home because the kids have now gone, it's a wonderful opportunity to reflect and be open for new things. Take the time to see what it is you want from life. Go out, take a bath, learn something new, meet up with your friends more, take up a hobby.

Change is tough for many. As humans, we really want things to stay the same. We're creatures of habit – and so am I - even for small things. Even when I redid my kitchen, I kept going back to the place where my salad oils were, only to remember that they're now in a different place.

Oftentimes it's difficult to put your thumb on the fact that you are going through transition. It feels disoriented and perhaps sad. When I was steeped in the hard side of transition, in the fog, confusion and the loss of an old self, a new feeling very slowly emerged, of new possibilities and greater vividness and intensity of life, change swimming in something rich and exciting with new ideas and energy.

One of the things that made a difference and that made the exciting parts come to the fore, and allowed the harder parts to fade into the background, was taking care of myself, even in little ways. I spent a lot more time with the people I love and I started getting out a bit more. I loved to spend time outside, getting my head showered. I'm the sort of person who likes to go deeper into my being and investigate what's going on in my inner world, which helped me to gain clarity, re-frame myself and understand my experiences. Where we feel stuck can be shifted if we put our attention onto it.

Give it words

When you sit down to write about it or to talk about it, you may feel like you don't have the right words, like you don't understand a thing about what's going on. That's okay. Say that. And then see what words come next. The process is what brings clarity.

It's helpful to write your feelings down in a journal. Have you ever had the experience of writing down how you're feeling, or speaking it out aloud to someone else, and then feeling like as a result, it somehow lost its aliveness? Maybe you told a friend about a previous experience and then suddenly felt like it lost its magic. Or you told someone about a new idea you were feeling super passionate about, only to find out afterwards that you felt inexplicably less passionate about it?

There is great power in forming words around things. When we use language simply to give words to our present moment experience, we tap its power as an accelerant of movement, a way out of being stuck. It can move us forward. And it helps you to release your feelings around things, moving and de-activating them. It moves something from being formless and unprocessed in us to something processed, drawn out of the ether into form. It then takes on a new shape in us, an evolved form, or it simply moves onwards, allowing space for the next energies to arise within us. It feels like we move through something, like we get through a struggle or a possibility.

I once was sitting with one of my best friends over a glass of wine during the autumn holidays and it popped out of my mouth that I wanted to do something I had never thought about before. This made me start thinking about what I had said, it gained energy and in the end, I realized what had been spoken through me. It was a weird experience. Like the truth had been obscured, lost in rationalization and in unsubstantiated arguments within my head, and nevertheless drawn forth and made into a piece of reality. It's a powerful way for truth to reveal itself and let itself be heard.

That's not the only power of language during times of transition. For me, naming my experience, putting concepts and words to it also gave my mind and my ego enough of a foothold that I then could allow transition to happen in a different way. And it offered me a way to validate and connect with others around my experience, which in itself was healing.

If you're feeling blue, don't be hard on yourself. Talk about it with the people you love and be open to support and letting your life unfurl again where a part of it stopped when your (first) child was born. I realize from interviewing many parents, that this subject isn't often a topic, yet many people go through this stage in life and we could learn a lot by talking to others who've already gone through the same experience. Instead of feeling like a fish out of water, it's great to get together and talk about how we feel. Even admitting how you feel is a great start, it will help you become more centered and relaxed with what's going on. Your story may trigger something in someone else.

Offer thanks and gratitude for all the ways the attachment to your kids has served you. After letting go of the emotional attachments change happens to bring with it, joy can follow. Joy can flush out whatever else you may be feeling, whether it's loneliness, fear and the other "stuff" that is no longer serving you.

Stop the mind chatter, and talk. If you think you don't know how to dive into the change in front of you, your intellect is the last thing you should latch on to. Have faith. Have courage. Keep breathing. And simply know that the next chapter of your life is unfolding effortlessly. This time of your life is even the perfect time to grow and to thrive.

Be honest with yourself

Truth is the pillar of change. Whenever we explain away our behaviours, or sugarcoat the truth, we pay the consequences, usually in the form of illness or drama. For example I had three boys and a husband and I simply went along with what my family wanted to do, which were obviously things that boys and men wanted to do. This entailed going to football matches to cheer them on, sports events, watching films they wanted to see and later drinking beer together, even though I, as a woman, was really missing out on things women do, like cooking together, riding or chatting as only women can do. Don't misunderstand me, I love each and every one of my males, but there was a definite deficit of female energy in our house.

I believed that if I didn't participate in what they wanted to do, no one would want to be with me. Though this belief was largely unconscious for most of my life, I have now sifted through this mud long enough so that the belief and the behaviour it birthed has gone – from my life and my body. In fact, after my children left home, I questioned a lot of things in my life to find out the truth for myself. While the truth may hurt, it will set you free.

To help yourself find your own truth, here are some good questions to ask yourself:

What's my daily life like right now?

What feelings are in my heart right now?

What am I grieving?

What feels attractive and appealing?

What have I been missing?

Embrace change

Many of us panic when faced with change and we try to control things, even try to fix things in order to resist it. But often that control just serves to reinforce our deep-rooted problems. At a certain point it's good to surrender to what is and just stop trying to control the outcome of everything. Otherwise our bodies, including our digestion and our nervous systems all get stuck in rigid patterns which eventually invite disease, behavioural problems and disability.

Change is the nature of life.

Movement and change happen permanently. When I meditate, there's a constant flow of changing senses, thoughts and states of being, which I love to perceive. It's the spacious, precious timeless being in the movement of life. This continues with our weather, the changing of the seasons, and with the cycle of life and death. The cells in our body are constantly dying and being renewed.

We grow older and wiser. Growing old comes on its own, we don't have to do anything to make it happen. The thing is, we don't have to see ourselves as being old. I find this thing of getting older really strange, as I don't feel older in my head, yet my body is changing. It's becoming a little rounder here and there. My skin is changing, as are my hair and my hormones. I don't think of myself as being old just yet, and I have no negative attachment to the fact that the years are creeping up on me. I like my face, I like the wrinkles around my eyes. The nice thing about it is that with my life experience, I do feel a lot wiser.

Being in the menopause is something I have come to relax into and accept. Of course it has its consequences, and it's my reality at present. I can look at myself and see what's happening. That's important.

I don't have the feeling that my life is almost over. I don't cry and want to be the young person I used to be. I don't mourn for the glances of men and I also don't feel invisible. I like to allow unusual, colourful and exciting things into my life, which has nothing to do with my age. I am interested and alert to people and to life.

Yes, I do tend to ask myself more often: "Who am I now?" With this process of transition there can be emptiness, disorientation, an in-between time, a not knowing who you are with no idea what the future will be like. It's like being in an in-between, neutral zone, which can be hard to sit and wait through. In actual fact, this transition may have started long before your children left home.

A friend of mine realized that long before her daughter left, she was hardly at home anyway. It's a part of growing up that the kids choose to be with their friends more than with their parents. They're searching for themselves, and at the same time the parents are finding out who they are.

Being in such a process, I felt quite off track at times. When you're stuck in the middle of it, you don't always realize that you're going through it. It's not just the external situation, it's an internal change too, which can bring a new beginning with it, where new ideas can move you forward until you have a new way of being. This can at first cause confusion. It has been difficult for me at times to deal with the everyday commitments. When everything is changing, it feels like being in quicksand, or sometimes in free fall. This sort of challenge does things to us.

Come out of hiding

We don't need to retreat fully from the world around us. There are many methods we can use to hide from immanent change. This may be food, alcohol, drama, or any other addiction. It could also be emotional blame and projection, which simply disables us from having a more meaningful relationship with someone.

When you get down to the nitty gritty of the things you are hiding from, you can be sure that an old pattern in your life will blow up and disappear. But not telling the truth and living a lie is far worse over time. Sometimes coming clean requires seeking support. It's worth it, as you will feel a sudden release of toxicity from your body, and with that you have the freedom to flourish and blossom.

Practice forgiveness

As I mentioned earlier, forgiveness is liberating. We all have our history, we have all had our traumas in life, yet there are sure to be situations in your life that haven't been dealt with emotionally, where you have shut down and not been able to feel what has been going on. The body and the mind have a really good method of protecting themselves from hurt, which in the long run can turn out to be unhealthy.

Surely there have been people in your life you have held grudges against. Surely there have been times when you have turned away in an argument instead of speaking out, when speaking out would have done you good. There are always underlying reasons for this. There may be people in your life you need to forgive for things which happened, even your children.

And very often the person you most need to forgive is yourself. To forgive yourself for whatever judgments you hold, simply say these words silently, or even better, out loud in front of a mirror: "I forgive myself for judging myself for... (fill in the blank)".

Face your fear

Although it's terrifying to bring a child into this world, because we don't know what the world is going to be like for them or if we will fail them as a parent, we don't know if we will be able to catch them should they fall. We don't know if they'll forget how to be happy, how to look at the stars, sing, read and love. Injustice terrifies parents. We are scared that the world won't be a safe and healthy place to live in. We are scared that the world will just whisk our children away.

And when it does, the fear doesn't go away. It doesn't stop.

We have to take tiny baby steps ourselves to learn to trust that the world will now take good care of our children.

Embrace your disappointments

Life often doesn't take us where we think we should be going to. We often have an ideal picture of how it should be. We also often compare ourselves to others and wish that we could be more like them. If you have been staying at home to look after your children, chances are you will have envied the mothers who have been out working, enjoying a career. And if you have been busy building up your career alongside bringing up your children, chances are that you would have loved to spend more time with your children. Chances are there are many precious moments you think you have missed out on.

Maybe there was the time when you couldn't go to the school fete or to the dentist with your child, when you felt that you should have. This causes disappointment in you and perhaps also in your child. You have done your best with the given circumstances. No-one is perfect, so there's no need to think that another parent has done any better. There will always be shortcomings we feel disappointed or guilty about.

It's best to let go of the past, forgive yourself and heal. It's then that we can learn to love so much more.

Be yourself

As a mother, I was afraid of being successful at my work when my children were small, as I didn't want my children to feel left alone. It seemed irrational. I recognized that this fear of success was a misconception. What I was really afraid of was abandonment. The "fear of success" indicates that earlier in life I learned to associate success with loss. But it had roots in very real situations that happened to me very early in life. My mother was a successful business woman, and worked long hours and travelled. I missed her a lot. And I didn't want my children to feel as I had.

It's important to understand this on a personal and cultural level, because when we understand it, we can release the hold of an ancient pattern that has kept us as women down for centuries.

Underneath the fear of success can also be memories of the abandonment that you have experienced in the past as a child during the moments when your joy somehow triggered your mother's/parents' anger, fear or jealousy. That is how we learn to associate our own personal joy with a loss of belonging. So we make ourselves small to fit in.

I don't think we're afraid that we're "powerful beyond measure" as Marianne Williamson describes in her famous quote. I think the child within us is afraid of the permanent banishment that ownership of this vast power would imply.

Parents cannot completely prevent children from ever experiencing moments of fear or lonesomeness. However, they can empathize with them consistently, so that over time, the child develops a predominant, overall sense of safety. Empathy is key. Empathy is more possible from adults who grieved enough about their own history that they don't avoid their child's pain as a way of avoiding their OWN pain.

On a cultural level, we have equated female power with abandonment. This is a cultural echo of that original scarcity of feeling abandoned by mother. Broadly speaking, men have feared that women who are conscious of their power will abandon their roles as nurturers. And patriarchy has taught men to disown their own nurturing abilities, encouraging them to seek nurturing mainly through sex.

Society's need for a subservient female, unaware of her power, is our deeper collective need to find a mother who won't abandon us. It's a projection of our traumatized inner children who are longing for an inexhaustible mother who isn't coming. I feared being successful in my work, and ultimately I didn't want to become someone who becomes abandoned either. The lonesomeness that we fear when we imagine future success is an inner echo of the terrifying lonesomeness we already experienced in the past. The inner mother emerges as we grieve and learn how to mother ourselves consistently. It's a skill that can be learned. If we fail to grieve and learn to mother ourselves, we risk passing along the mother wound to the next generation.

Culturally we need to grieve. Personally we need to grieve.

On a personal level, success can remind us of our ability to trigger our mother's fears and the resultant threat of abandonment by her.

Did you ever hear any of these growing up?

"Don't compliment her. She'll get a big head." (To others who compliment you)

"Stop looking at yourself." (if looking at your self in the mirror)

"Who do you think you are? I'll bring you down to size!"

"Don't complain, so many people have it worse than you." (When expressing needs)

For women of past generations, success as a woman was equivalent to abandonment.

As little girls and young women, a lot of us were taught that our value comes from supporting others and diminishing ourselves in the process. We were taught that "good girls" don't "shine too brightly". We also saw how this belief damaged and depleted our mothers.

We learned to view our success as a betrayal of the unspoken rule to put pleasing others ahead of our own needs.

The good news is that the thing we fear most has already happened. We can never be abandoned to that degree again. As adults, we'll never be that helpless, vulnerable or dependent again on others in the ways we were as children.

We may have experienced emotional withdrawal or physical abandonment or violence. Our conscious mind may not remember the details. Our nervous system remembers this clearly. And it throws up the warning signals of "fight, flight or freeze" when we allow ourselves to contemplate levels of success or happiness that were considered traitorous in our families.

Our freedom lies in our courage to grieve the traumatic lonesomeness we ourselves felt as children. The fear of success fades, allowing us to step more freely into our potential. It can take time to work up courage to feel this grief fully. We do it in increments. It's a primordial, existential grief and it may feel like you're grieving for countless generations before you. And the relief you feel as the grief subsides opens up a whole new world.

It's like the tectonic plates of your being shift finally into place opening up possibilities that were previously invisible to you.

The truth is that the bigger the change is that we want to experience in our outer lives, the bigger the inner change that must take place first. To make these big, lasting changes, we must go to the point of causation, to our past where painful patterns were put into place in our childhoods. In grieving the cause, we open up new horizons that were impossible before.

There will be discomfort when we cease deriving our sense of value from pleasing others.

We'll be uncomfortable because we're releasing an ancient pattern that feels so familiar. And others will be uncomfortable because the buffer between themselves and their "stuff" will be gone. They will be forced to be in contact with their own pain. Your ability to endure the discomfort of this change is critical. Remember that this discomfort is temporary. The important thing is to withstand the guilt feelings that may arise and not allow them to direct your behaviour. Use the guilt as a stimulus to more fully affirm yourself.

With consistency, the discomfort will give way to a profound sweetness of being, of feeling the joy, of belonging to yourself. As a woman radiating with the permission to be her full self, you offer a powerful "frequency of possibility" for others. You become the fulfilment of an ancient dream of your fore-mothers - a woman who is an individual, a woman unto herself...

Transition for the Kids

All transitions are composed of an ending and a beginning. In-between this is a zone of disorientation, neutrality and re-orientation.

For our children, the ending is the time when they let go of the old thing before picking up the new one, and not just outwardly, but also inwardly. They let go of the definition of who they are, in this case being children living under the roofs of their parents' houses.

They go from dependency to being independent. Leaving home is a huge part of growing into an adult. The end of childhood comes, although it could have ended earlier with the first sexual encounter, with the menstruation, or with another incisive experience. Some children were forcibly evicted from childhood through circumstances beyond their control, for example, when they were forced to take on the role of looking after younger siblings, or even a parent who was incapable of fulfilling their role.

Upon leaving home, a child's identity takes on something new.

They go from being so-and-so's child to establishing a separate identity. This development has been going on since birth with a series of roles and experiments as the son, the daughter, girlfriend, boyfriend, shy, outgoing, talented, sporting, etc.. They have eaten the food bought and cooked for them. They have lived with their parents and have turned to them for help. They have rejoiced in the human family. Now they go their way on their own. Becoming independent and finding their own place in the world entails a symbolic slaying of the parents and the dependency that had once been necessary. The small circle of the familiar childhood world has opened to embrace new experiences and impressions. The more they have been allowed to do things for themselves, the more successful they can be at being an independent human being.

Change will be easier for some children than it is for others. Some don't feel the need to go too far away from home, if the circumstances allow it, they will stay quite close. Some feel the tug of life and the need to leave. Some don't want to be the last ones in the family to be at home, and plan their exit by staying away and pushing against authority in any way possible.

As the initial excitement, and perhaps a little panic of being separate from the parental orbit begins to wane, new questions arise, and the emphasis slowly shifts from leaving something to finding and fitting into something else. For some youths, rebellion has been taking place against the way of living they have gotten used to at home. A separate and independent life starts constructing itself, there is a discovering of the own individual lifestyle, and their own relation to things, where the parents will have played a model role.

This can begin even before they leave home, in testing themselves in their own boundaries, seeing how far they can go. One mother told me of the conflicts she had with her son before he left home. There was a lot of anger, blame and inner turmoil within him, which he let out on his mother, who was intelligent enough to realize what was going on. When he left home and found himself, their relationship changed for the better again.

I remember this phase extremely well myself. I left home and moved immediately to a new country, where everything was different for me – the language, the food, the things I bought to eat, the culture, and lots more. It felt as if I'd been thrown into water and had to learn to swim. I didn't drown and I learned a lot in a very short period of time.

Meanwhile the parents are usually sitting at home worrying about their child, wondering if they are homesick, are maybe weeping as well, perhaps just like it was when they started school and felt so out of place, if they are getting enough vitamins to eat, and are managing to fend for themselves in the way they would like to take care of them. Often the first night being alone as a parent is spent sitting in bed weeping.

I know of one man who wasn't able to cope with the thought that his daughter had left home and was probably sitting with nothing decent to eat. So he cooked a meal for her and went round to her flat with it, expecting to surprise her with it and keep her from starving, only to find that she was sitting happily with a group of friends in her place, enjoying the delights of cooking together. She wondered if her father was alright. Needless to say, he left after saying hello and goodbye.

Or perhaps the parents are glad to see the back of them, a wicked thing to say, and which also happens for reasons known only to those who are feeling this way.

Of course it's daunting for the parents when the day comes when the kids stand on their own two feet. On the one hand they have been looking forward to this day since giving birth, and on the other hand parents do grieve. It's also daunting for the children when they notice that their parents cry. They are looking forward to getting out in life and meeting new people, the world seems to open at their feet, which they grasp with natural curiosity.

It's great that they can expand their territory, and also that they can come back again to the safety of their parents any time they want to. Indeed it's healthy for the human system to learn that the feeling of fear out there can be balanced with safety, and that life is a safe place to be in where the batteries can be recharged again. This is a healthy moving back and forward between active and relaxed, and active and relaxed.

For anyone, the safety to relax is important. Of course this continues when the kids go, and a safe base encourages the movement from freedom to intimacy and back again, much like baby animals will move further and further away from their mother over time, and return to her, finding their internal centre this way. I have found that our kids have grown to appreciate family occasions such as Christmas, Easter, weddings and special birthdays for good get-togethers, when they love coming home.

When the inevitable looms, in a lot of civilizations a ritual happens to celebrate the entering of a new phase in the life of the young adult. In our society we can herald this in by honouring the one who leaves as a child and returns as an adult in a celebration with the family. This honouring allows the kids to leave with a sense of appreciation on both sides, and they know how appreciated and loved they are, that they are being held in love whilst they start flying, just as they were when they made their very first independent steps or learned to ride their bicycles.

Learning from others

Up until now I've mostly told you about my own story of stepping into change. And because this book is not about me, I interviewed many people who have gone through, or are in the middle of this stage in their life, when the children are in the throes of leaving home. The stories I have chosen are all different, just as mothers and fathers are all different and have different ways of dealing with transitions in life.

A lot of useful things revealed themselves from these talks, which I summarize towards the end of this chapter. First of all, here are what others have been telling me. All names have been changed for the comfort of keeping privacy.

Julia

Julia has two children. Her eldest daughter has already left home, and she is preparing for her other daughter to leave in the near future. They have always lived together with a lot of other people.

Her children were born at the time when she lived in a shared house, so there were always lots of children and adults to play with, share activities with and talk to.

A few years ago they moved to a flat in the city when the relationship with her partner broke up. It wasn't too bad when her first daughter moved out and they keep very good contact. Now she notices that her second daughter is preparing herself for leaving, and she is hardly ever at home, spending more and more time with her friends and at her boyfriend's place. She knows that this is a necessary phase of dis-attaching, yet Julia is having problems adjusting due to the fact that she is not at all used to being alone. It scares her a little and makes her feel unwanted.

On top of that she has the feeling that her career isn't going anywhere at present. She seems to barely cover the minimum financial essentials. So there's not much left to be able to squander it on pampering herself in any way, which she admits would most likely make her feel better, at least temporarily. And she knows that self-care is a major issue for her now. She would like to be able to treat herself and eventually have a new partner.

Sven

Sven has a boy and a girl and has been a single parent since his son, the youngest child, was two years old. His own parents have been great in supporting him in his role as a father. He is an extremely independent person, is very social, has made a lot of money in his life and has always managed to give his children a comfortable place to live in, a good education and all that they needed.

Sven's children have always adored and appreciated him and they were the ones who did the housework of their own free will, and helped him when he needed help with anything in or around the house. They became quite independent from an early age, they were able to cook for themselves and both of them were very close to each other and seemed to look after and stand up for each other from their teenager years.

Sven had several changing partners during the time when the kids were growing up, several of whom moved in with them for a while. To a certain extent they took on the role of a mother for them until each relationship finished.

Sven fell in love with a woman who lived in a different part of the country and they realized that a weekend relationship wasn't what they wanted. It was also too much travel for them, so it was Sven who decided to leave the children behind in their home, and moved away to be with his girlfriend. The children were aged eighteen and twenty at that time. The daughter's boyfriend moved in with the two of them, which offered them an extra feeling of security, as he was a down-to-earth guy who loved to take care of them.

It was easy for Sven to leave, as he felt that it was the inevitable thing to do. He wanted his children to be independent. The house was there for them, and when he came to visit, there was always somewhere for him to stay.

The two children first of all got on with their life, it wasn't new for them that their father was impulsive and good for a surprise, indeed they loved him for it. It was only after a while that they realized that having a house and looking after it wasn't what they wanted. The chores and the work in the garden became tedious;

they felt overwhelmed with the situation and had other priorities in their life, so they decided to move also. They found a flat for the three of them.

The bond to their father remained strong and it was actually years later that they were all able to talk about how they had felt then. The father had really missed his children and had felt quite homesick. His new relationship didn't last and within a few years he moved back near his children again. His daughter had missed her father very much indeed, she had felt abandoned. His son also, although neither of the children admitted it at the time.

Now there are grandchildren and Sven enjoys spending time with them and does his best to be a great granddad.

Gudrun

Gudrun has one son. When he was small, she left his father as the relationship hadn't been working. When he was fourteen years of age, after having a turbulent relationship with his mother, he went to live with his father, who seemed to keep him on a longer line than his mother had been doing.

This was quite difficult for Gudrun to accept, but she let him go and in doing so, also gave up a large part of the control she felt that she had over her son. She knew in the back of her mind that he may come back again, so she got on with her life. With a feeling of huge regret and guilt, she watched as her son changed over the years, becoming a drug addict, and then a dealer. She felt completely powerless. The father didn't want their son to move back in with her, although he was also feeling overwhelmed with the situation. Gudrun felt that she had completely failed as a mother, and as a wife, putting the blame on herself that her son had developed the way that he did.

A lot of self-help work for Gudrun showed her that her son felt even more scared than she or her ex-husband did. That seemed to be a turning point for them. Acceptance and love, instead of judgment and control allowed them to approach their son in a completely different manner. A lot of forgiveness took place within the family, which helped everyone to feel better. The son was able to accept his parents too and his life took a turn for the better. There now is a strong bond between all of them, something which Gudrun's son had always been searching for from the most important people in his life.

Daniella

Daniella has three children — two girls and a boy, and is happily married. She is a psychologist and a very warm, intelligent person. She likes to look at the problems in her life as they show themselves, no holding back and no pushing things away. Her first daughter has left home to go to university in a different city.

Before she left, they had a mother-daughter chat about how it had been to be a mother and a daughter, and what they would have done better if they could do start all over again. Her daughter admitted that she had always wanted a mother who would absolutely smother her in love, always be there for her, cook her everything she wanted and cuddled with her. Now this is what often happens. Children see mothers who are different than their own, and see the benefits of having a mother who is different, and want to experience this kind of mother love, not that it's better or worse. What you don't have is what you want, it's just the same with your hair or your figure.

So Daniella agreed to become the mother her daughter wished for before she left home. She was allowed to stay in bed and be waited on hand and foot, she was cooked for and spoiled. She was cuddled and smothered with motherly love... until her daughter told her to stop it after two weeks. She couldn't stand it any more and longed for her mum to just be herself again, be the independent mother she had known and loved. They had got what they wanted and learned to appreciate each other so much more. The inner child in her daughter had what she felt had been missing and now she was ready to fly the coop. Which she did after a wonderful farewell party with all of her friends and family was given to send her on her way with much love and good wishes.

And of course there were tears in parting. And Daniella did feel lonely and missed her. Life went on and she got used to it and appreciated her "grown up" daughter when she came home on holidays. They found that they were now able to talk and relate differently to each other. The new life situation of her daughter brought a lot of new aspects into their relationship.

On the other hand, Daniella is someone who is never bored, always has fun with the things she does and has her two feet firmly on the ground in her career. She has a man who supports her and a circle of women around her to whom she can always turn to talk something through, which immensely supports her and carries her through difficult stages in her life.

Gaby

Gaby is married and has three children, the oldest two are twins. At the time of our interview the youngest one had already left home and the twins were preparing to leave. Gaby had the feeling that this was happening in a natural way.

When her first child left, she felt as if a part of herself had been amputated. Suddenly there seemed to be a lot of empty space around her, and she almost sold the house. Being a mother who likes to protect and take care of her kids, they were the centre of her life. She has always felt a pull between her work and the children, which almost ripped her apart at one time. She always tended towards the children, they were the number one for her.

Gaby recognized that she covered her feeling of loneliness up with the kids. The loneliness is beginning to show up again now that there is a transition taking place in her life, and she is able to face it better than she had in past times. She has found it very helpful to be able to talk to other mothers in her women's circle about what's going on in her life, especially when the eldest one left home, to get things off her chest and hear about other womens' experiences and how they dealt with it.

This transition took a few months. She saw that she could visit her son, who became a father at the young age of twenty. She was always there for him and they both went through this change together. She now enjoys her role as a grandmother with the feeling that there is a healthy distance between them all. She finds it does her and her kids good that she is able to back off when she feels the urge. The primal feminine, the caring and the nurturing mother remains. When her son comes to visit, she loves to run into the kitchen to cook for him, she finds that there is great meaning and comfort in eating together.

At the same time, she has to see in which ways she can nurture and respect herself in this phase. She loves to go out more often, and parallel to that, she likes to stay in and connect with herself. There is a strange mixture of brute force and freedom at present. Often the increasing feeling of freedom causes fear and anxiety to arise within her. She now works freelance. Although she tries to hold on to familiar structures here, she also tries to let go and give her control over things up to her inner guidance, which is a new feeling for her.

Her husband is moving through a transition with his work too, and has taken on a new job in a different city, where he will have to live during the week. At the same time, her twins are moving out, and she is at the stage where she tells herself that she has to bear up and persevere and be patient. On the other hand, she is used to taking action when she has the chance to do so, so she is currently finding this balancing act rather difficult to handle. And she knows that something new is maturing within her.

Gaby finds herself thinking a lot about the past. She feels guilt now and again that she wasn't able to control her anger and the aggression which was part and parcel of it when the kids were growing up. It seemed to sneak out at times and the family unfortunately took the brunt of it. She has felt that she was incapable as a mother. Thankfully a great deal of healing has been able to take place, accompanied by some truthful communication between them all. Indeed she has been blaming herself more than she was blamed for her actions - an agonizing state of mind to dwell in. Her own parents have been excellent examples for this behavioural pattern. In recognizing this, and in feeling her anger, and questioning how she can deal with it in a healthy, feminine way instead of allowing it to sneak out and hurt others, she realizes that there is a huge potential in the power of the emotion itself. Anger is now welcome without her taking it out on someone else.

In the near future, she will inevitably be alone a lot more. She already feels that she is in a sense "unemployed". She used to be so full of life, and the life around her is going. At the same time, within this process of detaching, a new vision is growing. The old function was very fulfilling. The transition still feels a little wobbly. It's being tolerated and she notices that change is happening inside of her.

Gaby's relationships with her children have changed. Even though she admits to thinking that everything can be dangerous for them out in the big wide world, even though there are times when she tries to hold on tight to them, she is also able to offer them good advice, and can withdraw and let them get on with it themselves. With her husband she is able to talk about these things, and he also is able to share how he feels. Even though he is a quiet man, when she asks him, and is patient, he is able to tell her how he's feeling with the situation. There are a lot of new things happening in their relationship. She has the feeling that they are more aware of each other and of what they both need, being able to be there for each other. They are becoming closer. After all, they hardly know what a life together without the children is like. The children were born in the early stages of their relationship.

Diana

Diana has a boy and a girl, she is married to their father. The children left home one after the other within a couple of years.

Diana says that this transition went really well. She found it very important to accompany her children into independency, especially when problems and issues arose for them. It was also important for her and her husband to be present as a couple for them. This all happened without any crisis for her, she has the feeling that she was able to let them go with joy. In saying that, she believes that she lives her life a little differently than a lot of other people do. Both her and her husband work from home, so there is always someone there, even though the kids have gone. They are both the kind of people who not only do a lot of things together, but also alone for themselves. They give each other space for other people in their lives. So there was already a feeling of deep fulfilment in their lives before this transition took place. Now the kids are doing well and Diana notices that a new life is beginning for her too.

Their first letting go was when their daughter left to go to Australia for a year. Being on the other side of the globe it was clear that they couldn't hop onto a plane and visit her for a weekend. Indeed there was no visiting at all done in this year. The relationship between them all changed for the better. Before she had left for Australia, there were clashes and arguments.

With her son there has always been a feeling of closeness, he is a sensitive person. In her present role as a mother, she sees her kids as grown-ups. She doesn't feel the need to define this role, she finds that she doesn't have to see if they are okay each and every day, but she is there when they need her. Before they left, the children were quite independent and were already going their own ways.

Diana has always told herself that when she reaches fifty years of age, and the kids are gone from home, she will do something for herself, and that it will be easier. She admits that the children are the most important thing in her life. She has no feeling of separation from them, indeed she feels a deep connection with both of them. Now everyone is doing their own thing even more. Her husband has more time for his friends and she has more time to do the things she loves, like being in seminars and learning more about herself and others.

When they do come home for a while, she doesn't feel the need to fuss over them or molly-coddle them. She's contented with things as they are, and can watch as everything unfolds effortlessly.

Sabine

Sabine has one son and has been a single parent for most of their time together. The question of where, how and in what way she would like to live presented itself to her years before her son ever left home. And she found the answer in her vision to make a project on a Portugesian island when she retires.

She has always lived with her son, and when he fell in love and married a girl from a foreign country, still being in his apprenticeship and not earning very much money, they decided that the best thing would be if they all lived together for a while. The flat was changed around a little, so that the newly-weds could have their own space. This worked well for them all, and Sabine liked having her daughter-in-law around.

After three years, the need to be alone grew for the couple, so they looked for and found a very small flat which they could call their own. Her son was just about to take his exams, so there were hopeful new times coming for him and his wife. Financially Sabine was able to help them out at the start, and she also helped them look for a flat. The process of letting his mother go was indeed an emotional one. Her son set clear boundaries on his mother and vented his anger on her to the state where she had to set her own boundaries and tell him when it was too much. Which was accepted, and she believes that this was part and parcel of his own process of letting go. At first he refused to take anything out of her flat to furnish their new one. There were things she offered them, as she knew that she had enough for herself, and planned to move into a smaller flat, reducing her space from 120 square metres to 36 square metres, to help her save for her retirement plans.

Being alone, she felt good, she was able to make arrangements for herself and concentrated herself on her work and her future plans. She was in Portugal as often as she could when she had time off. Her family came to visit her there, but they found out that it's not the way they want to live, so it's clear that this is and remains her own vision, and it's a new phase in her life which she enjoys and is looking forward to more in the future, when she will live on her island within three to four years.

All the same, she feels that she will of course remain being a mother her whole life long. Her son now says - "actually, I'm able to talk to you about everything". Now and then he's able to express his affection for his mother. He brings her flowers on his own birthday as a token of his gratitude, and thanks her that she gave birth to him. This makes her proud and happy.

Sabine is looking forward to being a grandmother as soon as her son finds a steady job. She is visited a lot by her son and daughter-in-law. And they know that they will have to come to the island to visit her in a while, she will not be able to be a grandma who lives round the corner.

She believes that the transition was so effortless for her because she had her own vision before her son left home.

Jane

Jane has two daughters and her family is a very close one. Her husband adores her. She has a lively personality and likes to take on challenges. She is busy within the church and loves travelling.

Both daughters have already moved out of the house. The eldest one doesn't live too far away. She remained living at home when she went to university, and her boyfriend practically lived there too at the time. So she was at the uni during the week and home at the weekends, which made the transition a gradual process. Now they are married and there is one granddaughter and another grandchild on the way, so they get to see each other often. The grandchild is absolutely doted upon.

When her second daughter left for university she felt horrible. They accompanied her to her new place, a short flight away, and saw that her new flat was so horribly dirty, and they thought that it wasn't the best of places to leave her in. But her daughter was fine, she was independent and she grew up. And it was only a flight away. When she up and moved to Australia with her partner afterward to work, Jane was heartbroken. She sobbed for weeks on end, as did her other daughter, who regrets already that her sister won't see much of her children while they are growing up.

Jane deals with this by organizing holidays to go and see her daughter. They have a great time together, and keep regular contact by skyping, texting and on the phone.

Since the kids left they have downsized their house. She finds that she is occupied with the care of elderly parents, as well as having a full-time job, which has sort of taken over from looking after the kids. There has been no guilt about anything at all done as a parent. She is able to talk to others, especially to her own sister about how she feels, which has helped her a lot in this new phase.

Her relationships with her daughters aren't any different than before they left, they all like themselves as people and they are always kind and loving towards each other. She realizes that they left home as children and are now adults. Jane feels that she has become a lot closer to her husband now, they do more together and have more time for each other.

Jane never really used to question her life at all, until she developed a severe illness not too long after her children had left, which she has now successfully recovered from. The result of which is that she would like to take an early retirement to do more of what she loves doing. And that is travelling and seeing more of her daughters, whom she admits that she misses terribly. She feels that they still need her, and with the family being so close, she wants to enjoy their company as much as she can.

Barbara

Barbara has two sets of twins and as a mother has always had tons to arrange and take care of. She feels that she grew into this role quite well.

Now that they have all reached the age of leaving, there are two stages where two children are leaving the house. The first set of twins moved out at the same time and went far away together. There was still contact with them of course, and Barbara felt that she could easily push her emotions aside by concentrating on the other two children.

A girl and a boy, the other twins remained. Then the boy moved out first and the girl is currently preparing to leave. They are going their separate ways, not like the other twins who decided to stay together. The boy needs his space and doesn't want to have much to do with his family at present.

She has downsized and lives with her daughter and her husband. Her own mother isn't well, so her attention and care is now directed at her, which has taken over caring for the kids. Nevertheless she feels devastated with the thought that they are almost all gone, and admits to having problems dealing with it. She keeps herself extremely busy to compensate, and always says that soon she will have time for everything she ever wanted to do, with tears welling up in her eyes at the same time. It's difficult for her to talk about her situation and face what's happening.

Conclusions

From talking to a lot of parents, some important points have crystallized. It may be of help for you to know them.

It has helped parents to go through this stage of transition in their life when:

- they have a vision for their life before the children leave home,

- they are able to talk to others about what is going on in their outer and inner life,

- they have a good relationship with their partners, with whom they can express their feelings and share this transition in a healthy way,

- they understand their children and are there for them, supporting them when necessary,

- they keep good contact with their children,

- they give themselves time to grieve if necessary, and allow space for new to develop organically.

A lot of parents seem to go from looking after their children to looking after their parents in the last years of their life. Nevertheless it seems to be important for all of them that they find a way to take care of themselves and live their own lives.

What comes now?

Alan Watts, a British-born American philosopher, writer, and speaker, said:

> "The only way to make sense out of change is to plunge into it, move with it, and join the dance."

I couldn't agree more.

So what comes now? The obvious change contains practical things, like deciding not to buy more food than you need for yourself. At the beginning of my own transition, I found that I was putting much too much food into my trolley at the supermarket, out of habit. I found that the housework I had been doing became less. Three cheers for that, it gave me time to concentrate on lots of other things.

As long as the children are at home, we're a family, and we have something important to do together, which is to parent the kids. No-one wants to stand in their way. It's just that when they're gone, if we're not parents any more, the question pops up, who are we?

To parents, the children always seem to remain to be their little children. The caring of the brood is a survival mechanism, which can be compared to the instinct of self-preservation. It's very important for parents, which explains the reason why some parents give themselves up in their intentness of doing the best they can. It often seems odd that an elderly woman looks upon her fifty-year-old son as being a child, and yet it does happen. Parents always remain parents, no doubt about that. Being parents, we may be scared of the transitions the kids are facing when they fly the coop, we may long for our own freedom, and we may try to cling to the past. Whatever, a wound will be made, and nevertheless it's healthy to move on.

You will learn a lot in your transition. Life may slow down for a while, at least it will seem so on the outside. Your inner life will intensify. You will find yourself first of all in a neutral zone. From a kind of emptiness which results, you will find that the emptiness is a container for intense growth. This may create the need to define your relationships anew. It may also cause you to change your role with your partner, with your children, your work and to use your time differently.

This can be challenging, as it's not respected in our culture to be in a neutral zone. We have no patience and feel uncomfortable when you don't know who you are or what you want to do next. The temptation will be there to add more things into your life to accommodate the shifting taking place. However, it's important to feel the need to let go of the old before the new enters into your life. There may be a feeling of waiting in the wings for a while, confusion and unsureness.

It's important to take care of yourself, allowing the stuff that's shifting to be welcomed, as I mentioned in chapter four. After all, we don't know what it's like to take care of this newly emerging version of yourself just yet. So in the absence of this clarity, be gentle with yourself. Don't rush. Give yourself time for contemplation and creativity. Be with the people you love, and with those who inspire you. Go easy on yourself. Start saying no if you mean it. Writing, talking, just naming it moves you through any blockages you may have. Start a ritual such as lighting a candle for yourself or meditating to give yourself space for your transition. Pay attention to synchronicities, clues and signs. Keep a folder with ideas and projects in it that you'd like to do. I go through mine at regular intervals. Sign up for a class to do something new. For me, it was taking the swimming lessons I had always wanted to take. You may find that a dream pushed aside comes up for you, which is nudging you to take another look at. Think of what would be unlived in your life if it ended today. Follow the energy. Make only short-term provisional commitments for a while to see where you are being guided to move towards in your life.

Sometimes all we need in order to change our reality is a little wisdom, spoken to us with gentleness and a pure heart. Trusting in the process is important. To help you, I'd like to offer you a powerful Lakota prayer, which I love. The Scared Space mentioned in it is the place of stillness, of the space between exhalation and inhalation, the balance between the heaven and the earth, the neutral zone.

Lakota Prayer

Great Mystery,

teach me how to trust

my heart,

my mind,

my intuition,

my inner knowing, the senses of my body,

the blessings of my spirit.

Teach me to trust these things

so that I may enter my Sacred Space

and love beyond my fear,

and thus walk in Balance

with the passing of each glorious Sun.

At the core of this timeless wisdom is the word "trust". When did we stop trusting ourselves? When did we start giving that special power away? In many ways the path is a process of re-establishing that trust that resides within us, just waiting to be reactivated.

If you feel that your energy is depleted, as transition is truly hard and energy consuming, do whatever it takes to recharge your batteries. This could be little things, the everyday things that do us good, the moment-to-moment, day-to-day experiences that replenish our spirits enough to help us get along.

Many parents will be noticing that there aren't so many opportunities to be giving so much of themselves any more. Many have to learn how to start receiving again. This can be easier said than done, as many of us find lots of reasons not to be able to receive things in life, most especially love. This is worth taking a deeper look at. So learn to nurture and love yourself here. Take some time to meditate. If you don't want to sit still whilst doing so, take a walk in nature. Simply take the time to breathe in and out fully through your nose - this stimulates the parasympathetic nervous system. Do whatever supports you and allow the emotions of pleasure, generosity and receiving to flow through you regularly.

My children have always been a big inspiration in my life. I love remembering all the unique things they said and did, and they love reminiscing too. They continue to amaze me, even now, or especially now that they've grown up. Their awareness and belief, especially when they were small, that anything is possible, is an inspiration for how we could all live our lives. As parents we've tried to do our best. It may not always have been right, but at the time, it was the best we could do.

Upon listening to many parents, a lot of them mentioned that they have started to feel and look older a lot quicker now that their children have left home. All of a sudden there is a change in their bodies, as if the young dynamic side of them went out the door with their children. Children think freely and remain open to learning. They have less fear about what others may think about them or their creativity. They have a natural state of joy and need no reason to be happy. They embrace who they are; we need to get back to this state of being open for new things in our life.

It's all so important to have new orientation for yourself, at home, perhaps in your relationships, in your work and your life too. This new phase can offer women a whole new look at their femininity. The phase of the crone, the wise woman commences at this time in life. The primal femininity emerges stronger than before, and shows a different aspect of itself. Women are confronted with themselves and their own needs, the acknowledgement of their changing bodies. A lot is falling away, the role of the mother is changing, as does the social performance which goes with it. The grip of caring for others can change to looking after elderly parents, which brings about a change of role. The advice giver emerges, a role respected in older cultures much more than in our present one.

You may notice that you're feeling stuck, unhealthy or miserable with an area in your life. This often happens when you take the time to reflect upon your life, as you do when a lot of the daily chores aren't necessary any more. And it's good, because it's a chance to change for the better. And yes, a lot of marriages do break up after the kids leave home. The time may be right to move on and see what else life has in store for you, just as much as the time may be right to improve a relationship.

When the realization arises that there is something wrong in your life, if something is stressful, be it in a relationship, at work, or with your personal health, instead of focusing on it, use it to pivot and shift the position. Because when we focus on what's wrong, it becomes more complicated to do what's right. That doesn't mean that we should ignore what's wrong. We can use it as an impetus for change, recognizing that it can prevent positive change if we dwell on it instead of taking the necessary steps. You know that nobody finds a better job just by complaining about the bad one. No one stops overeating by resolving not to. You can't improve a relationship just by fuming about how awful it is.

So what we need is a replacement strategy. Which is nothing less than out with the bad and in with the good. Replace what you don't like any more with something else you feel positive about. For example, instead of wanting to eat again when you find yourself standing at the fridge door, go out for a walk. If you want to get out of a bad job situation, find a better option. The way to improve a relationship is to cultivate and expand on what's already working for you in it instead of dwelling on what's not.

You may want to retreat a little, or a lot, and ask yourself what you don't like about your current situation. Detox from the noise. Get to know that inner voice again. Learn to enjoy your own company again. Whether it's your job, your health, your relationships, whatever, ask yourself how it makes you feel, think and perform. Life is nothing but change, the part of yourself that wants to remain the same isn't realistic.

What would you like to change about your current circumstances? Now that you're clear on what's wrong and why, it's time to decide what you would like to change about it. Clarity on this point is essential because the negative feeling or situation serves as the trigger for positive action. Being in a neutral zone is an exquisite time for new insights. Here are a few questions which may help you:

What do you want more of in your life?

What would you like to accomplish?

What have you imprisoned that is crying to be free?

Is there something fulfilling and important that you should focus on?

How can you live a significant life?

Is there a suppressed dream you would like to consider again?

How could you change? Once you know what you want to change, you're ready to formulate your replacement strategy. Identify a positive action you could take in response to the negative trigger. Stay flexible and open for all possibilities.

As we have discovered from those who have been through this transition themselves, including myself, who had no idea about anything, consulting and talking to someone who understands you is very beneficial. Talk with other women who are in your situation. If you are a man, talk with other men. You're not alone. The possibilities for this are greater than ever before. If you don't know who you can turn to, ask around, seek support groups, a coaching group, go online to find blogs and forums. And don't stop until you find the person or group you need.

Change may not come easy. I thought in my passage that I had finally found all the answers, only to have my questions change – also a part of my process. I now realize of course, that had I not done it all as I did, I would not be the woman I am today. It hasn't all been smooth sailing, yet I feel that I'm now closer to being who I am, and I have the right to be happy.

Beneath the surface there may be fear of change, as we do move into the unknown when we change. We can have the feeling that we cannot control our lives, and emotions may run high during these times. So a realistic assessment of your situation may be necessary. Try to centre yourself and ask yourself a key question: Is this a problem I should fix, put up with, or walk away from?

Unless you can answer this question clearly and rationally, your vision will be clouded by stressed-out thinking. Without knowing it, you will act under the influence of negative emotions, old habits or impulsive behaviour. Patience makes sense here. If you find yourself facing a world which seems to be full of fears, illusions, wishful thinking, denial, distractions and conflict, it's necessary to dig deeper inside of yourself. The problem will never be solved with the energy it was created from. Repetitive thinking gets us nowhere, old conditioning keeps us at the level of yesterday's outworn choices, obsessive thinking and stalled action. The truth is that you have more than one level of awareness, and at a deeper level there is untapped creativity and insight. Try to reduce your stress with meditation, reflection, contemplation and prayer. Whatever you like doing, the first steps begin inside of you.

Clarify your situation to enable you to act on what you are clear about. And enjoy.

Give yourself permission

Perhaps you need permission to let your children go their ways? Is there a reason you are trying to hold on to them? It may be that you are afraid of losing your identity, or that you know that you have to take on responsibility for your life and your own happiness now?

There have been times in my life when I've felt stuck. It has been useful to enquire if I need permission from someone in my life – from my mother, my father, my partner, my children, from society or even from myself to do something.

Don't kiss your children goodbye with a heavy burden of knowing that you feel lost without them. It's not their issue to worry over. Work through it.

I know that there were times when I hid behind my kids. It was easy to do that. I didn't have to say much, or be much else than a hen clucking over her chicks. Many women lose their own identity when the kids are small, or they push them out of the way because there doesn't seem to be any time to get on with just being yourself. It's often an easy way out. But it all catches up on you when the kids have gone, and you are posed with the question of "What now?".

Feel in to your being and be honest with yourself, if there is any permission needed from anyone to let your kids go. It may be from your own mother who had a hard time letting you go. It may be from your partner, who also needs a mother figure in his life. It may be from your child, who thinks that he will lose you if you let go. It may be from society as you have fitted into this role of being a parent for so long. It may be from yourself in order to get on with your life in a different way.

Celebrate yourself

It's so important that you acknowledge yourself for having the courage to face your own personal mud. Celebrating yourself ends the cycle of shame and pain. When the dirty work's done, your strength, beauty and transformation can sweep through you, allowing you to reap the benefits and wisdom of your journey.

Choose someone to celebrate with you, someone truly capable of understanding and supporting you in all that you are.

And delight in the miracle of your children. You created those miracles. You've gotten them ready to go out into the world, support themselves, and become productive members of society. That's HUGE! Pat yourself on the back, well done.

You've spent decades caring for everyone else. It's your turn now!

Epilogue

I was lucky enough to use the tools I have acquired with my Journey work and coaching techniques to help me get through this stage of transition in my life. I have had to learn to engage in emotionally honest and often terribly frightening conversations with myself and others. We all have gaps in our comprehension of the world and we all have holes within ourselves too.

There may come a time in your life when you might want to process your pain and get to the root cause of it, perhaps in a professional setting. It's wonderful to take accountability for going out there in the world and filling in your own gaps.

I hope that you find your own teachers. If you feel called to work with me, I'd love to assist you by walking you through whatever is necessary, filling in the missing parts and finding the right path for you.

You will find more self-help books by me on my website, take a look at www.ruth-bleakley-thiessen.com/books/

Much love,

Ruth

About the Author

Ruth Bleakley-Thiessen is a communication designer, a Journey Practitioner, a coach, an artist and an author. She has coached thousands of people one-on-one and in workshops, most of them women, helping them to evolve, empower and express themselves in their own authentic way.

Her first book was published in 2000 with the Christa Falk Verlag in Germany (*Die Lehren der Engel*).

She is from Ireland and lives in the north of Germany.

Other books by the Author

More books written by Ruth Bleakley-Thiessen can be found on her website: www.ruth-bleakley-thiessen.com/books/

Titles include *Woman Rise and Shine.*

To receive more information about her books and more you can sign up for her free newsletter here and receive a free e-book:

www.ruth-bleakley-thiessen.com/free-ebook/

Made in the USA
Middletown, DE
08 September 2022

73470991R00056